MW01060223

Vancouver is a your positive change. For good-looking, this is striving for the cutt innovate and improve, the city, gathers leading graphic designers, tech entrepreneurs, writers, filmmakers, artists, and musicians close. A place where beauty and truth is observed, imagined, and interpreted, Vancouver is poised perfectly between East and West, and drawing the best from these worlds, its influences ripple worldwide.

CITIx60: Vancouver explores Canada's largest seaport city in five aspects, covering architecture, art spaces, shops and markets, eating and entertainment. With expert advice from 60 stars of the city's creative scene, this book guides you to the real attractions of the city for an authentic taste of Vancouver life.

Contents

Before You Go

BASIC INFO

Currency
Canadian Dollar (CAD/$)
Exchange rate: US$0.7 : $1 : €0.7

Time zone
UTC/GMT-8
DST +1

DST begins at 0200 (local time) on the second Sunday of March and ends at 0200 (local time) on the first Sunday of November.

Dialling
International calling: +1
Citywide: 604, 778, 250, 236
Toll-free: 800, 844, 855, 866, 877, 888

Weather (avg. temperature range)
Spring (Mar-May) 11°C-17°C, 52°F-63°F
Summer (Jun-Aug) 12°C-25°C, 53°F-77°F
Autumn (Sep-Nov) 10°C-17°C, 50°F-62°F
Winter (Dec - Feb) -10°C-8°C, 14°F-44°F

USEFUL WEBSITES

Route planning for Metro Vancouver
www.translink.ca

Public bike share system
www.mobibikes.ca

Lifestyle news & entertainment weekly
www.straight.com

EMERGENCY CALLS

Ambulance, Fire or Police
911

Non-emergency police
+1 (604) 717 3321

Consulates
Australia   +1 (604) 694 6160
China   +1 (604) 734 7492
Mexico   +1 (604) 684 1859
UK   +1 (604) 683 4421
US   +1 (604) 685 4311

AIRPORT EXPRESS TRANSFER

YVR <-> Vancouver City Centre (Canada Line)
Trains / Journey: every 6-20 mins / 24 mins
From Airport: 0507-1256 daily, One-way: $9
From Vancouver City Centre: 0500-0107 daily,
One-way: $4
thecanadaline.com
www.yvr.ca

PUBLIC TRANSPORT IN VANCOUVER

SkyTrain
Westcoast Express
Bus
SeaBus
Bikes
Taxi
BC Ferries

Means of Payment
Compass Card
Credit card
Cash

*A single fare allows unlimited rides within 90 minutes. Compass works across all modes of transit.

PUBLIC HOLIDAYS

January	1 New Year's Day
February	Family Day (2nd Monday)
March/April	Good Friday
May	Victoria Day (Monday before May 25)
July	1 Canada Day
August	British Columbia Day (1st Monday)
September	Labour Day (1st Monday)
October	Thanksgiving Day (2nd Monday)
November	11 Remembrance Day
December	25 Christmas Day, 26 Boxing Day

Galleries, museums and some shops are likely to be closed around Christmas and New Year's Day. Smaller shops may close on public holidays.

FESTIVALS / EVENTS

January
PuSh International Performing Arts Festival
pushfestival.ca

April
Make It Vancouver
makeitshow.ca

May
DOXA Documentary Film Festival
Doxafestival.ca

June
Queer Arts Festival
queerartsfestival.com
Jazzfest
www.coastaljazz.ca

July
Indian Summer Festival
indiansummerfest.ca
Vancouver Folk Music Festival
thefestival.bc.ca

August
Powell Street Festival
www.powellstreetfestival.com

September
Hapa-palooza
www.hapapalooza.com
Vancouver International Film Festival (thr. Oct.)
viff.org
Vancouver Fringe Festival
Vancouverfringe.com

October
Vancouver Art/Book Fair
vancouverartbookfair.com
Vancouver Writers Fest
www.writersfest.bc.ca

November
Eastside Culture Crawl
culturecrawl.ca

Event days vary by year. Please check for
updates online.

UNUSUAL OUTINGS

Pink Floyd the Sea Wall (June)
velopalooza.ca

Wild Whales Watching
www.whalesvancouver.com

Ferry Graveyard
Use caution. Entering is considered trespassing.
Cooper Ave., off Lougheed Hwy, west of Mission

Vancouver Brewery Tours
vancouverbrewerytours.com

Movies in the Morgue
vancouverpolicemuseum.ca

SMARTPHONE APP

Buy Local Eat Natural
We heart local

Street food hunt
Street Food App

One-way, on-street car hire
Car2go, Evo Car Share

Real time public transport app
TransitApp

REGULAR EXPENSES

1 Liter of gas
$1.26

Domestic letters / international airmail
$0.85 / $2.50

Gratuities
Diners: 15–20% for waitstaff & bartenders
Hotels: $1–2 @bag for the porter
Licensed taxis: 10–20%

Count to 10

What makes Vancouver so special?

Illustrations by Guillaume Kashima aka Funny Fun

Nature, architecture, and art fuse to make Vancouver a distinctive city inspired by its own history while also being influenced by those coming and going from its port. A diverse population constitutes an assortment of quintessential Vancouver experiences. Whether you are on a one-day stopover or a week-long stay, see what Vancouver creatives consider essential to see, taste, read and take home on your trip.

1

First Nations Culture

Traditional & contemporary art
Museum of Anthropology (#23) & Vancouver Convention Centre West (#4)

Aboriginal art showcases
Lattimer Gallery & Douglas Reynolds Gallery, *lattimergallery.com, douglasreynoldsgallery.com*

Stories told by Musqueam people
Musqueam Cultural Centre
www.musqueam.bc.ca

Wood carvings, textiles & clothing
Khot-La-Cha, *khot-la-cha.com*

Aboriginal cuisine
Salmon n' Bannock,
www.salmonandbannock.net

Squamish & Lil'wat Culture
Squamish Lil'wat Cultural Centre
slcc.ca

2

Local Brews

R&B Brewing
www.randbbrewing.com

Brassneck Brewery
brassneck.ca

33 Acres Brewing Co. (#54)
33acresbrewing.com

Main Street Brewing Co.
mainstreetbeer.ca

Strathcona Beer Company
strathconabeer.com

Strange Fellows Brewing Co.
strangefellowsbrewing.com

Faculty Brewing Co.
www.facultybrewing.com

Parallel 49 Brewing Co
parallel49brewing.com

CRAFT Beer Market
www.craftbeermarket.ca

3

Vancouver Flavours

**Salmon, Sablefish,
Spot prawns (harvest season: May)**
Ocean Wise partners,
Restaurants in False Creek, Gyoza King

Fish & Chips
Fish Counter, Howe Sound Brewing,
Edible Canada, Go Fish

Salad
Field & Social, The Birds & the Beets,
Farmer's Apprentice, Royal Dinette,
Fresh Roots

Vegetarian & Vegan
The Acorn (#41), Nomad,
Chau Veggie Express, Meet on Main

Ice-cream
Earnest Ice Cream (for Whiskey
Hazelnut flavours), Rain or Shine,
Bella's Gelato, Casa Gelato

Chocolate
Beta5, Chocolate Arts, Koko Monk, East
Van Roasters, Thomas Haas, Thierry

4

Multicultural Eats

Chinese
Torofuku, Bao Bei, Kirin,
Sunny Spot Café

Japanese
Yuji's from Japan (#44), Hime,
Toshi, Kishimoto, Irori,
Sushi Den, Guu

South & Southeast Asian
Indian: Vij's (#42); Cambodian:
Phnom Penh; Filipino: Kulinarya;
Burmese: Amay's House;
Thai: Talay Thai, Maenam,
Sawasdee Thai

Ukrainian
Ukrainian Village

European
German: Bestie; French: Les Faux
Bourgeois, Salade de Fruits Café

Mexican
Tacofino, La Taqueria

5

Cafés & Coffee Roasters

Matchstick Coffee Roasters
Favourite local independent
www.matchstickcoffee.com

Revolver Coffee
One of the first and best
Third Wave Coffee counter
revolvercoffee.ca

Liberty Bakery (#40)
www.liberty-bakery.com

Café Medina
With a Mediterranean-inspired menu
www.medinacafe.com

Timbertrain Coffee Roasters
Train-themed space for zesty
espressos
timbertraincoffeeroasters.com

Propaganda Coffee
Snug spot also for hot chocolates
www.propagandacoffee.ca

6

Markets

Granville Island Market
Gorgeous produce, great baked
goods, delis & local crafts
granvilleisland.com/public-market

False Creek Fisherman's Wharf
Daily catches, summer only
www.falsecreek.com

Mercato Italian Market
Artisanal produce, crafts, music &
outdoor pizza oven
italianculturalcentre.ca

Trout Lake Farmers Markets (#36)
Delicious food, fresh produce, and
East Vancouver charm

Nat Bailey Winter Farmers Market
Food & wholesome local fun
eatlocal.org/markets/nat-bailey

Vancouver Flea Market
A great way to escape the rain
www.vancouverfleamarket.com

7

Arts & Design

An artist-run centre since 1973
Western Front Society, *front.bc.ca*

Novel modern ballet
Ballet BC, *balletbc.com*

**Designers' favourite for furniture,
house goods & books**
Vancouver Special, Inform Interiors
shop.vanspecial.com,
informinteriors.com

Antique wares for home & office
JoJo's Place, *jojosplace.com*

Local clothing on Main Street
Eugene Choo, Smoking Lily,
Bird on a Wire, Front & Company

Independents in Gastown
One of a Few (#25), Oak + Fort,
Old Faithful Shop, Livestock

Canadian made buttons
Button Button, *buttonbutton.ca*

8

Music & Literature

Local bands & experimental music
The Lido (#56), VIVO Media Arts Centre
vivomediaarts.com

Vintage & boutique gear
Rufus Guitar Shop & Exile Guitars
rufusguitarshop.com, 21exile22.com

New, rare, used records
Red Cat Records (#31), Zulu Records,
Neptoon Records, Dandelion

**Where Nirvana, David Bowie &
Duke Ellington had played**
The Commodore Ballroom
www.commodoreballroom.com

Books by Vancouver or BC authors
The Paper Hound (#30)

Impressive art book selection
Or Gallery, orbookstore.orgallery.org

Used novels, real travel books
MacLeod's Books, 455 W Pender St.

9

Closer to Nature

Easy hike (2.5hrs)
Lighthouse Park–Cypress
Mountain–Dog Mountain (St
Seymour) / Deep Cove

More challenging hikes
The Stawamus Chief in Squamish

Consume Vancouver air
In Stanley Park & along the Seawall

Boat up the Indian Arm
Take in the city from the sea with
snacks & wine from Granville
Island's arsenal shop
www.boatrentalsvancouver.com

**Kayak to Bowen Island,
in False Creek or Deep Cove**
*www.ecomarine.com/rent,
www.deepcovekayak.com*

Swim & lie in the sun
Third Beach, Jericho Beach

10

Beyond the City

**Old Buntzen Power Station
by Francis Rattenbury**
A popular film location up Indian
Arm, where nature, technology
and architecture converge

**Catch a seaplane
to one of the Gulf Islands**
www.gulfislandseaplanes.com

See art, architecture & nature
Audain Art Museum (#21)

Pick local berries
Try Westham Island and combine
with a visit to George C. Reifel Bird
Sanctuary for a view of the mighty
Fraser River Delta, in spring or
summer

Sea to Sky Gondola (#9)
Enjoy the scenery from the drive
to the Gondola base all the way to
the Sea to Sky top deck

Icon Index

 Opening hours   Admission

Address   Facebook

Contact   Website

Remarks

 Scan QR codes to access Google Maps and discover the area around each destination. Internet connection required.

60x60

60 Local Creatives x 60 Hotspots

From vast cityscapes to the tiniest glimpses of everyday exchange, there is much to provoke one's imagination. 60x60 guides you to 60 locations favoured by 60 of the city's keenest tastemakers.

Landmarks & Architecture　SPOTS · 01 – 12 📍

With origins in First Nations longhouses, Vancouver's architecture is renowned for the work of local and international legends and, recently, an emphasis on green buildings.

Cultural & Art Spaces　SPOTS · 13 – 24 📍

Vancouver is a port city rich with influences, however, traditional and contemporary works by indigenous artists define the local spirit.

Markets & Shops　SPOTS · 25 – 36 📍

From artful handmade items to regional foodie flavours, Vancouver's markets and shops offer items that truly represent the diversity of the city.

Restaurants & Cafés　SPOTS · 37 – 48 📍

Constantly innovating, and with West Coast's freshest ingredients, chefs, and restaurateurs, Vancouver's foodie paradise has multiple versions of your latest food obsession.

Nightlife　SPOTS · 49 – 60 📍

Whether it's from drag show glitter, the gleam of a cold one, or the city's reflection on the surface of False Creek, Vancouver nights are sure to sparkle.

Landmarks & Architecture

Nature-inspired, iconically visioned and greening with style

Framed by the Coast Mountains and nestled in the Salish Sea's northernmost inlets, Vancouver's architecture and landmarks are intimately connected to their natural surroundings. The cedar long-houses raised by Northwest Coast First Nations people 3,000 years ago were uniquely suited to the famously rainy climate – the influence of these original post-and-beam structures continues in West Coast Modern buildings such as Arthur Erickson's stunning Museum of Anthropology (#23). Another indelible influence is the Seawall, a car-free path tracing the water's edge from Stanley Park to many of the city's most coveted neighbourhoods and landmarks. Hop on one of the city's cute Mobi bikes to trace the architectural mutations of this relatively young city: the Beaux-Arts-style Pacific Central Station's 1912 opening propelled the city's current growth, Gastown's cobbled streets host many an Edwardian, and the Burrard Bridge is an Art Deco remnant. Keep an eye out for the boxy Vancouver Specials, sturdy economical homes from the 1950s now nostalgically beloved. Sometimes called 'See-Through City' due to its current glass-towered density, Vancouver's post-Olympics trend is towards varying skylines and world-class green buildings.

Ann-Marie Fleming
Filmmaker, writer & artist

I have lived all over the world but made Vancouver home for the mountains and ocean. My work deals with themes of family, history and memory. I travel a lot but am quite a homebody when in town.

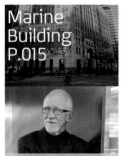

Marine Building P.015

Roger Hughes
HCMA Architecture + Design

Roger Hughes takes pleasure in solving problems with design. As HCMA's founding partner, he creates architecture that contributes to a strong, healthy and socially diverse society.

Jeff Khonsary
Publisher & editor

Jeff Khonsary works behind Fillip, a platform for critical discussions on contemporary art, and art book publisher, New Documents. Edited work includes *Institutions by Artists*.

Sylvia Hotel P.014

Simon Fraser University P.016

Claudia Schulz
Milliner

I wear many kinds of hats and have lived in Gastown with my husband and son for the last 15 years. Nothing beats the fact to be surrounded by mountains and ocean at the same time.

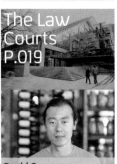

The Law Courts P.019

David Gunawan
Owner, Farmer's Apprentice

Named Chef of the Year by 2016 Vancouver Magazine Restaurant Awards, David Gunawan is a champion of locavores. He also owns Royal Dinette in downtown Vancouver.

Suzanne Ma
Journalist & author

Suzanne Ma's stories have appeared in *The Wall Street Journal* and *Bloomberg Businessweek* alike. She authored *Meet Me in Venice* (2015), a book about the Chinese immigrant experience.

Vancouver Convention Centre West P.018

Dr. Sun Yat-Sen Classical Chinese Garden P.020

Derya Akay
Artist

Derya Akay's work involves food and experiments with new recipes. Born in Turkey, he now works in Vancouver. He's the winner of Portfolio Prize's Emerging Artist Award in 2016.

The Totem Poles @ Stanley Park

Jordan Abel
Writer

A Nisga'a writer from Vancouver, he is the author of *Injun* (2016), *Un/inhabited* (2014), and the 2013 poetry book, *The Place of Scraps* (winner of the Dorothy Livesay Poetry Prize).

Alvin Kwan & Vince Lo
Founders, Studio Faculty

The duo started Studio Faculty in 2012. With a focus on branding, web and print design, and art direction, Faculty hopes to make a valuable impact for the city through their work and vision.

LightShed

Sea to Sky Gondola

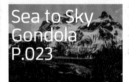

Hana Pesut
Photographer

Globally known for her dual portrait series where couples of all kinds trade looks, Hana Pesut also works as a digital marketer and DJ. She published the *Switcheroo Book* in 2013.

Hastings Racecourse

Reece Terris
Artist

A VIVA Award recipient, Reece Terris interrogates people's relationship with the built environment by altering the expected experiential qualities of objects and places.

Gordon Nicholas
Photographer

Gordon Nicholas finds a balance between his personal and commercial works. He documents his daily life and curates it into a journal of good times he had with his skate rat and road trips.

Bloedel Conservatory

Lynn Canyon

1 Sylvia Hotel
Map E, P.106

An English Bay icon, this brick-clad hotel has inspired songs, poems, and a popular children's book series about its resident cat, Mr. Got-to-Go. Built in 1912 and named for the developer's daughter, this beloved heritage site continues to hold its own as an architectural landmark even as the city becomes awash with glass. The hotel's cosy lounge, opened in 1954 as Vancouver's first cocktail bar, is an unpretentious hidden haven from which to take in sights of the seawall and spectacular seaside sunsets. In the fall, the building's ivy-covered exterior flames with colour.

🏠 1154 Gilford St., BC V6G 2P6
📞 +1 (877) 681 9321
URL sylviahotel.com

"I used to live in its similarly vintage sister building, the Kensington. I love new, but I feel most at home in old. Come in the late afternoon and watch the sun set."
– Ann-Marie Fleming

2 Marine Building

Map G, P.107

When it opened in 1930, with brass-doored elevators moving over 200 metres per minute, the seaport city had seen nothing like it. Considered a close equivalent of New York's Chrysler building and a fine example of Art Deco-style architecture, the Marine Building features a grand entrance and intricate motifs of the city's nautical history throughout, making it a popular film location. Spend time taking in the impressive lobby modelled after Mayan temples and views from the second floor balcony. The office tower is also home to Tractor Everyday Healthy Foods, where one can pick up a delicious guilt-free lunch.

🏠 *355 Burrard St., BC V6C 2G8*

"Walk from the Neoclassical Royal Bank Building on Granville Street and sight buildings such as the Sinclair Centre and Norman Foster's Jameson House."

– Roger Hughes, HCMA Architecture + Design

3 Simon Fraser University
Map S, P.110

Built in the 1960s, Simon Fraser University's (SFU) Burnaby campus is a magnet for modernist enthusiasts and film productions alike. It's a bit of a trek (about an hour by transit, 30 minutes by car), but visiting the Arthur Erickson construction is worth the journey for the dozens of public art pieces and their world-class art gallery, if not for the mountain air. The Brutalist campus would begin Erikson's lifelong love affair with concrete. Additions to the grounds over recent decades have been done in a sensitive manner, keeping the overall aesthetic fairly cohesive. Make sure to check out the library and the Academic Quadrangle.

🏠 8888 University Dr., Burnaby, BC V5A 1S6
📞 +1 (778) 782 3111 URL www.sfu.ca
🔗 SFU Gallery: Room 3004, Academic Quadrangle, 1200–1700 (Tu-F)

"Bridge Beardslee's 1976 Energy Alignment Sculpture, Pyramid in the Golden Section in the Academic Quadrangle is a must see."

– Jeff Khonsary, New Documents

4 Vancouver Convention Centre West

Map G, P.107

Opened in time for the 2010 Winter Olympic games, with a six-acre living roof populated by native plants and four colonies of bees, seawater heating and cooling, and a fish habitat built into its foundation, the West Building amply earns its LEED Platinum designation and makes a striking addition to the waterfront landscape next to the original East Building. It is especially worthwhile to explore wide offerings of British Columbian and international art between the two buildings, including numerous large installations by First Nations artists Susan Point and Joseph Wilson, as well as Douglas Coupland's killer whale sculpture *Digital Orca (2009)* in the Jack Poole plaza.

🏠 *1055 Canada Pl., BC V6C 0C3*
☎ *+1 (604) 689 8232*
URL *www.vancouverconventioncentre.com*
🎟 Tour schedule & price vary

"Start your walk from the Convention Centre and walk, bike or skateboard around the seawall and Stanley Park."

– Claudia Schulz

5 The Law Courts
Map A, P.102

This Arthur Erickson design literally upends the concept of a highrise by presenting a skyscraper on its side. Housing the Supreme Court of British Columbia and the Court of Appeals, the complex is distinguished by a one-acre sloped glass roof symbolising publicness and three cascading waterfalls traversing the top of the central building. Take in the full glory of the complex and its greenscapes from the Vancouver Art Gallery's (#22) upper levels or café. The subterranean Robson Square hosts public ice-skating and other cultural programming, and is favoured by salsa and break-dancers during off-hours.

🏠 400-800 Hornby St., BC V6Z 2C5
📞 +1 (604) 660 2468
 www.courts.gov.bc.ca

"Also worthy of note is the urban garden designed by Cornelia Oberlander."

– David Gunawan, Farmer's Apprentice

6 Dr. Sun Yat-Sen Classical Chinese Garden

Map A, P.103

In conjunction with the Expo '86 extravaganza, the Garden was one of the first Ming Dynasty-style Chinese scholar's gardens on foreign soil. It is worth the admission to admire the superb Chinese carpentry, walkways, and the immaculately landscaped garden. Be sure to tag along for one of their free tours and help yourself to unlimited hot tea. Every season is a treat in this spot of quiet and beauty close to the city. Keep your eyes open for the turtles and, in late spring, the ducklings nesting under a shrub. The garden's summer concert series features beloved local groups.

🕐 1000–1800 (May–Jun 14 & Sep), –1630 (Oct–Apr), –1400 (Dec 24 & 31), 0930–1900 (Jun 15–Aug 31)
💲 $12/10/9   🏠 578 Carrall St., BC V6B 5K2
☎ +1 (604) 662 3207
🔗 vancouverchinesegarden.com
📎 Closed Mondays from November 1 through April 30, on December 25 & January 1

"This is one of the most beautiful spots in the city. Highly recommend you take a tour to learn about the Garden and all that it symbolises."

– Suzanne Ma

7 LightShed
Map G, P.107

Based on old boat sheds that offered repairs and shelters along the shoreline, this Liz Magor sculpture forges multiple connections with Coal Harbour's past. Magor's work notably explores themes of history and survival, and LightShed is a good exemplar of that notion, as a nod to the harbour's previous life as a shipyard. Cast in half-scale, the shed is perched on stilts and illuminates from within by night. A stroll along the seawall of Harbour Green park is rewarded with the discovery of more large outdoor installations, many of the notable ones rotating courtesy of the Vancouver Biennale.

🏠 *Harbour Green Park, 1199 W Cordova St., BC V6E*

"The whole thing is cast in aluminium, even the smallest barnacles. There are lots of details to look at."
– Derya Akay

8 The Totem Poles @Stanley Park
Map Q, P.110

The nine totem poles collected at Brockton Point are considered one of Stanley Park's top attractions. Located near the site of X̱wáy̓x̱way, a large First Nations village estimated to have seen three thousand years of inhabitance until its forced closure in the late 1800s, the serene setting of the totem poles is a notable visual reminder of Vancouver's origins. The last remaining indigenous Squamish family moved out of Stanley Park in 1935. The Rose Cole Yelton Memorial Totem Pole is erected in front of the site of their former home.

🖉 *Stanley Park main entrances: (1) 1970 W. Georgia St. (2) 2061 Beach Ave. (3) Lions Gate Bridge Rd. Park shuttle service: late June–early September, $10/5, www.vancouvertrolley.com/tour/stanley-park-shuttle*

"This is a great place to come check out how Vancouver strategically positions indigenous culture as, essentially, a tourist attraction."

– Jordan Abel

9 Sea to Sky Gondola

Map Y, P.111

A scenic hour's drive from downtown, The Sea to Sky Gondola is located in city of Squamish, and takes visitors to a point above and behind the beloved rock face known as the Stawamus Chief. Once above the clouds, test your courage on the hundred-foot long Sky Pilot Suspension Bridge while taking in spectacular views of Howe Sound, or take them in from the Summit Lodge and grab a bite to eat. Consider extending your time in Squamish by exploring adventures both on land and water.

🕐 May–Sep: 1000–2000 (F–Sa), –1800 (Su–Th), Sep–Apr: –1700 daily 💲 $40/38/25/14, Down ride: $15
🏠 36800 Hwy. 99, Squamish, BC V8B 0B6
📞 +1 (855) 732 8675 🌐 seatoskygondola.com
🔗 Last ride down departs at 1 hour after closing. Roundtrip shuttle from/to downtown available.

> "Great scenery from the drive to the gondola base, the gondola ride up and finally, the Sea to Sky top deck."
>
> – Alvin Kwan & Vince Lo, Studio Faculty

10 Bloedel Conservatory
Map U, P.111

Opened in 1969 in commemoration of Canada's centennial celebrations, this triodetic dome building is the country's largest single-structure conservatory. It hosts more than five hundred species of tropical plants and a resident population of more than one hundred free-flying birds. Strolling the nearby grounds reveals some of the best vistas of greater Vancouver, hidden gardens, and a number of sculptures including a Henry Moore. On snow days, the nearby slopes provide the city's best sledding. The nearby Seasons in the Park restaurant offers magnificent city views, especially at nighttime.

🕐 May-Aug: 0900-2000 (M-F), 1000-(Sa-Su), Sep-Apr: 1000-1700 daily
💲 $6.50/4.35/3.15
🏠 Queen Elizabeth Park, 4600 Cambie St., BC V5Z 2Z1
URL vandusengarden.org/explore/bloedel-conservatory

"The building itself is really unique and fun to photograph. It's a nice place to go when the weather is no good, which can be often in Vancouver."
– Hana Pesut

11 Hastings Racecourse
Map R, P.110

In operation since 1889, the Racecourse in Hastings Park is one of Vancouver's best throwbacks. Beyond the track is a gorgeous view of the North Shore Mountains, unchanged from the day it opened. Racing season runs between April and October, chiefly on weekend afternoons starting at 1.50pm, when locals can be seen showing off their best outfits. If visiting in summer, be sure to also make a stop at the century-old Playland park and summer fair nearby. For a slice of nature, check out The Sanctuary within Hastings park, or take a ten-minute walk to New Brighton Beach.

🕐 Hours vary with race days
🏠 PNE Gate 6 or 9, BC V5K 3N8
📞 +1 (604) 254 1631
URL www.hastingsracecourse.com
🔗 19+

"Check the racing schedule before you go. Dress up (not necessary at all but super fun!), eat hotdogs, view the horses before the race and bet heavy."

– Reece Terris

12 Lynn Canyon
Map O, P.110

For those looking to escape the city and are not afraid of heights, this is a great choice. A favourite amongst locals, it's a spectacular spot to enjoy raw natural surroundings compared to the touristy Capilano Suspension Bridge up the mountain. For those wanting to explore further, try the plentiful trails through the thick pine forests. Be sure to dress appropriately for a rainforest environment. And if you decide to go for a dip in the river, be aware of the cold water and the strong current.

🕐 1000-1700 (Jun-Sep), 1200-1600 (Oct-May)
🏠 3663 Park Rd., North Vancouver, BC V7J 3G3
🔗 lynncanyon.ca 🔗 By bus: take bus 228/229 from Lonsdale Quay to Lynn Valley Centre, then walk 15 minutes to the park entrance.

"Take the short hike on the other side to some fantastic swimming holes."

– Gordon Nicholas

Cultural & Art Spaces

Independent culture hubs and coastal northwest art

Art comes in many forms in Vancouver. Thanks in part to the city's Public Art Program, artwork can be found across the city, adding meanings to locations in unexpected places – look up while walking around town! Diverse arts events bring people together throughout the year, such as the Queer Arts Festival, the Eastside Culture Crawl, and the PuSh Festival, as well as celebrations of identity such as Hapa-palooza, Indian Summer Festival, and Powell Street Festival, to name a few. A good source to find out about shows and other happenings around town is the local publication, *The Georgia Straight*, available in print and online (*www.straight. com*). Find these events calendared in *Before You Go*. To set up a self-directed tour of the city's outdoor art projects, check out *www.vancouvermuralfestival.com* and City of Vancouver's Public Art website (*vancouver.ca*).

Institutions like the Vancouver Art Gallery (#22) and the nearby Bill Reid Gallery, as well as the Museum of Anthropology at the University of British Columbia (#23), are places where you can find works truly representative of Vancouver's past, present, and future. Vancouver galleries, both small and large, have a common goal of wanting to make art accessible and interesting to the public, and are keen to show off what makes Vancouver's scene distinctive.

Janice Wu
Visual artist & illustrator

I graduated from Emily Carr University in Vancouver with a BFA in 2013. My work addresses material culture, the everyday, and perceptions around symbolic and sentimental value.

Back Gallery Project
P.034

The Flats
P.035

Andy Dixon
Artist

I'm a painter, born and raised here in Vancouver. I currently work between New York and Vancouver. I'm represented by galleries in New York, London, Los Angeles, and Vancouver.

Margherita Porra
Founder, arithmetic

Margherita Porra is known for her innate talent in brand creation, cultural trend clairvoyance and pared down designs. Her experience chiefly lies in consumer goods categories.

Rennie Museum
P.036

David Arias
Graphic designer

I have a passion for adventuring our natural backyard here in BC, and documenting my jaunts via pictures. As for my design work, whatever it is, my goal is to make my subjects look 'cool'!

The Aviary
P.038

Presentation House Gallery
P.039

Yuriko Iga
Owner, Blim

Yuriko Iga was born in Winnipeg with Japanese parentage. She runs community-based art recourses centre, Blim, and works in Powell Street Festival's programming committee.

Birthe Piontek
Visual artist

Originally from Germany, Birthe Piontek moved to Canada with a MFA in 2005. She chiefly works with photography and her work explores issues around identity, womanhood, memory and loss.

Chan Centre for the Performing Arts
P.040

Courtenay Webber
Owner, The Future

I'm a creative director, designer, illustrator, writer, music freak and chanteuse behind The Future, a multidisciplinary design studio focussing on branding and identity for cultural clients.

Vancouver Public Library, Central Branch P.043

Susan & David Scott
Scott & Scott Architects Ltd

Set up in 2013, Scott & Scott notably uses locally sourced materials in their projects. The firm received The Architectural League of New York's Emerging Voices Award in 2017.

Lyle Reimer aka Lylexox
Makeup & mixed media artist

Lyle Reimer teaches for MAC Cosmetics in Vancouver by day, and designs creative looks by night. He finds beauty in odds and ends, and draws inspirations from everywhere.

The Rio Theatre P.042

Audain Art Museum P.044

Dylan Staniul
Partner, Burnkit

Born on the Canadian Prairies, Dylan Staniul has an obsession with old Porsches and orphaned vintage chairs. He always stays for one last drink because that's when the best stories come out.

Museum of Anthropology P.046

Meagan Albrechtson
Owner, Lolita

Meagan Albrechtson's magazine *Lolita* profiles inspiring creatives and entrepreneurs. She loves travelling to new cities, cycling the city, reading *Bon Appétit* and hosting dinner parties.

David Phu
Musician & multimedia artist

David Phu recorded as a member of City of Glass, photo-blogged for *Vancouver Cycle Chic*, and co-directed *Point of Inflection* and abstract movement video series *Panic Attack*.

Vancouver Art Gallery P.045

New Media Gallery P.048

13 Back Gallery Projects
Map C, P.105

Perched in Strathcona, an area where many artists and independent galleries call home, Back Gallery Project feels between a studio and a gallery, making a comfortable environment to take in new works. Monica Reyes founded the gallery in 2013 and runs the gallery's programme herself. Its solid roster includes emerging and mid-career artists who work in varied mediums, from the more traditional paintings and sculptures to the more experimental performances and spatial interventions.

🕐 1300–1700 (Tu–Sa & by appointment)
🏠 602 E Hastings St., BC V6A 1R1
☎ +1 (604) 336 7633
URL www.backgalleryproject.com

"This is my gallery representation!"
– Janice Wu

14 The Flats
Map B, P.104

Previously perceived as a dead space between East and West Vancouver, the former marshland in Mount Pleasant now acts as a connector between the two sides, via art. Over 15 of Vancouver's most important art galleries reside in the art district, including the much-loved Western Front Society, Catriona Jeffries Gallery and Monte Clark Gallery. Emily Carr University of Art & Design's relocation to the Flats continues to transform the area to a cultural and educational centre. Nearby, one can spot Vancouver artist Ken Lum's *Monument for East Vancouver* – more often nicknamed the "East Van Cross" – best viewed at night.

🕐 Hours vary with galleries
🔗 theflatsvancouver.tumblr.com
🔖 Galleries mostly close on Mondays and Sundays and welcome guests from noon to 5pm.

"Have a map on your phone handy because some, like Catriona Jeffries, have back alley entrances which are a bit hard to find if you don't know where to look."

– Andy Dixon

15 Rennie Museum
Map A, P.103

Martin Creed's 2008 neon art piece "Everything is going to be alright" mounted on the roof of the Rennie Museum is an uplifting sentiment. Yet it's worth pondering when a developer chose to house his private art collection in a struggling, impoverished, and rapidly gentrifying Chinatown. English-speakers with internet access will find it easy to gain free but appointment-only entry to the beautifully-restored heritage building and the impressive contemporary art exhibits within. Changing about twice a year, the collection unironically showcases works that address issues surrounding identity and social injustice. While the street-level entrance is small, the large gallery and sculpture garden above surprises.

🕐 By guided tour only (W-Th, Sa), booking required
🏠 Wing Sang Building, 51 E Pender St., BC V6A 1S9
URL renniecollection.org

"Book a tour and be treated to an entertaining and inquisitive guided tour of relatable and inspiring artwork. Be sure to check out the rooftop garden."

– Margherita Porra, arithmetic

16 The Aviary

Map D, P.105

Co-founded by designers Andrea McLean and
Stella Boyland, The Aviary seeks to foster a connection between creative individuals and the
public in the heart of flourishing Fraserhood.
The idea is underpinned by a design library and
an open, all-white space where workshops, re-
tail pop-ups, speaker series and art shows take
place. Their shop space is an extension of this
creative mandate, where member architects,
interior and graphic designers, photographers
and artists can be found knitting together after
hours. Feel free to set-up here to work with a
day pass or just drop by during business hours.

🕘 0930-1730 (M-F)
🏠 637 E 15th Ave., BC V5T 3K5
☎ +1 (604) 785 9282
URL theaviary.ca

*"It's Vancouver's first open studio dedicated to
supporting independent architects and designers. Be
sure to check their calendar for upcoming events."*
– David Arias

17 Presentation House Gallery (The Polygon Gallery)

Map P, P.110

Celebrated as West Canada's largest showcase of contemporary Canadian photography and media art for nearly four decades, the Presentation House Gallery has grown beyond the capacity of its original space and is anticipating its new waterfront location to open later in 2017. With prize-winning Patkau Architects leading the design, the new venue will add exhibition space to accommodate the large-format work of local artists such as Jeff Wall, Ian Wallace and Rodney Graham, and extra rooms for events, lectures and talks. The gallery's revamp will include name change, and the gallery will return as The Polygon Gallery.

URL *presentationhousegallery.org*

"This is an underrated gallery with high profile shows! Have a nice day trip to North Vancouver by SeaBus and enjoy good eats at the Lonsdale Quay!"

– Yuriko Iga, Blim

18 Chan Centre for the Performing Arts

Map F, P.106

The zinc drum tower of the Chan Centre is a favourite shooting location for sci-fi films like *Battlestar Galactica* (2014) and *The Fantastic Four* (2015), but in real-life it's a world-class stage that has welcomed the Dalai Lama and Yo-yo Ma, and sees the diploma presentation to thousands of freshly minted graduates yearly. Designed by Bing Thom architects, the building's 37-tonne acoustical canopy resulted in one of the tallest buildings on the University of British Columbia campus. The surrounding forest of cedars and rhododendrons masks this height and makes for serene lobby views during intermissions.

🕐 💲 *Hours & admission vary with events*
🏠 *University of British Columbia, 6265 Crescent Rd., BC V6T 1Z1*
📞 *+1 (604) 822 9197*
🔗 *chancentre.com*

"If you're up on the campus, make sure to check out other venues of UBC's Arts & Culture District. Most importantly, the Museum of Anthropology (#23)."

– Birthe Piontek

19 The Rio Theatre
Map J, P.108

A fixture in Vancouver since 1938, located in a rare Art-Deco art space, the Rio Theatre is a Vancouver treasure for its programming that features more than international and independent cinema. Its line-up of concerts, spoken word, burlesque, and comedy shows makes the spot a cultural epicentre for the popular Commercial Drive neighbourhood. Try to catch Paul Anthony's *Talent Time*, the variety show that has guaranteed a good laugh for nine years straight!

🕐 *Hours vary with show* 💲 $12/10
🏠 *1660 E Broadway, BC V5N 1W1*
📞 +1 (604) 879 3456 🔲 *riotheatre.ca*

"Drink white wine and munch a grilled cheese while watching a midnight screening with a rambunctious audience."

– Courtenay Webber, The Future

20 Vancouver Public Library, Central Branch

Map A, P.102

Co-designed by Sadie Architects and DA Architects & Planners, the spiralling cylinder of Vancouver's Central Library has become one of the nerve centres of downtown since its opening in 1995. Forming the entry foyer flanked with shops and cafés, the outer wall provides reading spaces and wraps around the main block where great reading materials are stored and free cultural programmes take place. Expect new community spaces to open on the top floors in 2018. Outside, Ron Terada's bulb-lit sign reflects the site's subtle complexity and its relationship with the public.

🕐 1000–2100 (M–Th), –1800 (F–Sa), 1100–1800 (Su)
🏠 350 West Georgia St., BC V6B 6B1
📞 +1 (604) 331 3603 URL www.vpl.ca

"It reminds me of Rome's Coliseum. I love to go there and dip into fashion books, be inspired not only by what's on the pages but the environment all around me."

– Lyle Reimer aka Lylexox

 Audain Art Museum
Map Z, P.111

Paul Wong's (p.087) rainbow neon installation in
the Audain's lobby is titled 'No Thing Is Forever.'
But if an apocalypse mysteriously vaporised
all the important West Coast art in Vancouver,
this suitably removed collection of British
Columbia art would represent salvation. Nested
in a conifer grove beneath the famed Whistler
and Blackcomb glacier mountains, this svelte
black Patkau Architects-designed museum
houses remarkable Northwest Coast masks
and major works by the likes of Emily Carr and
E. J. Hughes, donated by local philanthropist
Michael Audain and his wife. If First Nations art
has your interest piqued, you will also relish the
nearby Squamish Lil'wat Cultural Centre.

🕐 1000–1700 (W–M) 💲 $18
🏠 4350 Blackcomb Way, Whistler,
BC V0N 1B4
📞 +1 (604) 962 0413
URL audainartmuseum.com

*"Great for a day trip but it's best to combine with
outdoor adventure, so stay at least two nights."*
– Susan & David Scott, Scott & Scott Architects Ltd

22 Vancouver Art Gallery

Map A, P.102

Located in a former courthouse, the Vancouver Art Gallery's permanent collection is notable for major works by Canadian artists such as, the Group of Seven, Jeff Wall, Stan Douglas and Ken Lum, amongst other international artists. Curated with an eye towards deep local and global perspectives alike, the exhibits are often paired with excellent public programmes including the much-anticipated adults-only FUSE parties, weekly family programmes, artist talks, and dance and musical performances. The Gallery's steps are a popular space for public cultural celebrations as well as protests and demonstrations, but it's due to move into its new Larwill Park home by Herzog & de Meuron in 2020.

🕐 1000-1700 (W-M), -2100 (Tu)

💲 $24/18/6.50/by donation (Tu after 5pm)

🏠 750 Hornby St., BC V6Z 2H7

📞 +1 (604) 662 4719

🔗 www.vanartgallery.bc.ca

✎ Free guided tour: 1100, 1200, 1300, 1400, 1430 (Th & Sa), 1100 (Su)

"Beautiful building, interesting exhibits, with a great café and patio to enjoy a beer or glass of wine. Expect a big line and a busy atmosphere every Tuesday night!"

– Dylan Staniul, Burnkit

23 Museum of Anthropology
Map F, P.106

Escape the city to discover the Museum of Anthropology on the University of British Columbia campus. The museum has an unparalleled collection of First Nations art, and is a great introduction to local history and culture. Take your time and check out the historic treasures from all over the world stowed in the drawers and storage cases: masks, tools, bowls, jewellery and more. Walk around the site to take in the ocean and mountain views, not to mention the distinct post-and-beam inspired West Coast architecture by Arthur Erickson. On the ocean-facing side of the museum, a pond representing a coastal inlet, originally conceived by Erickson, was installed in 2010 and reflects surrounding structures, foliage, and sky.

🕐 1000–1700 (F–W), –2100 (Th)
💲 $18/16/13/10 (Th after 5pm)
🏠 6393 N.W. Marine Dr., BC V6T 1Z2
☎ +1 (604) 822 5087
URL moa.ubc.ca
🖉 Closed October 15-May 15 Mondays

"The museum's location sits on the UBC Endowment lands, which offer several lush forest trails perfect for a pre- or post-museum adventure."

– Meagan Albrechtson, Lolita

24 New Media Gallery
Map V, P.111

An intimate space dedicated to showcasing international multimedia artwork and pushing the boundaries, the New Media Gallery also features regular artist talks. Want to maximise your experience at this gallery? The friendly curators are keen to give tours whether you're alone or in a group. New Westminster is often referred to as the "Brooklyn" of Vancouver for its growing arts scene and initiatives such as LitFest New West and Music by the River, and is still secret to many Vancouverites. New Media Gallery is easily accessed via Skytrain.

🕐 1000–1700 (Tu–W, F–Su), –2000 (Th)
🏠 3/F, Anvil Centre, 777 Columbia St., New Westminster, BC V3M 1B6
📞 +1 (604) 875 1865
URL newmediagallery.ca

"It's in a huge, cool building, so take 30 minutes to explore the architecture. It's easy to find. Just look for the New Westminster Skytrain station."
– David Phu

Markets & Shops

Independent boutiques, farm-fresh markets, international inspiration

Vancouver's best shopping can be found in clusters of shopping areas featuring more independent stores than the big-names found in malls and on Robson Street. Part of downtown is Gastown, known for its designer shops for fashion and home interiors. Close by is Chinatown – a great place to find inexpensive wares for the home as well as items made by local artists (check out Blim on East Pender Street). Not far away is Main Street and Mount Pleasant, home to Antisocial Skateboard Shop (#27), Atelier St. George (#26), The Regional Assembly of Text (#29), and plenty of other interesting boutiques.

Many farmers markets can be found around Vancouver from May to October, and are a great place to feel community spirit and taste artisan specialties. Granville Island (#34) is a popular spot anytime of year, but especially busy during the summer. It features artist studios and a world-famous produce market amongst a picturesque waterfront setting. Just off the island, one can find high-end interior design shops and art galleries. Think Anthropologie, Eileen Fisher and Marion Scott Gallery in South Granville, and West 4th for outdoor and active wear, Zulu Records, Gravitypope shoes and clothing.

Kuh Del Rosario
Elmo's House Artist Residency

Kuh Del Rosario's practice spans from painting to sculpture. She started Elmo's House Artist Residency in Batan, Aklan, as a portal for the arts between Vancouver and the Philippines.

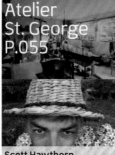

Atelier
St. George
P.055

Andrew Pommier
Multidisciplinary design studio

Ontario College of Art and Design graduate Andrew Pommier has worked with skate and snowboard companies such as Toy Machine and Girl. His work has appeared in Juxtapoz and Warp.

Scott Hawthorn
Co-founder, Native Shoes

A jack of trades, Scott Hawthorn chairs Native Shoes, co-founded Design Build Research and operates an orchard in Penticton. He tends to lead with intention but without expectation.

One of a Few
P.054

Antisocial
Skateboard
Shop
P.056

Fahim Kassam
Photographer & filmmaker

Born and raised in North Vancouver, Fahim Kassam currently works between Vancouver and New York. He has shot pictures and videos for Stussy, Inventory Magazine and sports brands.

The Regional
Assembly of
Text
P.058

Laura Byspalko & Sirish Rao, *Indian Summer Festival*

The co-founders of the annual omnivorous, multidisciplinary festival of the arts enjoys bringing worlds together. They live by the sea in Kitsilano and are out on the town six days a week.

Tracy Stefanucci
Writer, publisher & curator

Tracy Stefanucci lives between Vancouver and Stockholm. She is also the director of Project Space, founder of Vancouver Art/Book Fair, and managing editor of Hayo magazine.

Neighbour
P.057

The Paper
Hound
P.059

Gareth Moses
Radio host & record label co-owner

Gareth Moses is one half of More Than Human and hosts radio of the same name on CiTR. He grew up in London listening to Tubeway Army and champions experimental electronic music.

Chinatown
P.061

Anna Ling Kaye
Co-founder, Hapa-palooza Festival

Quill & Quire named Anna Ling Kaye one of seven who encouraged diversity in Canada's book industry in 2015. An established editor and award-winning writer, she co-produced CITIx60 Vancouver.

Steve Smith-Dla'kwagila
Artist

A true Vancouverite, I feel blessed to live here with my family. Through art, I hope to touch people's hearts and let them see First Nations artwork in a way they may not expect to see.

Red Cat
Records
P.060

Welk's
General Store
P.062

Armin Tehrani & Eunice Quan, *Co-founders, Priory*

The duo co-founded Priory with friends David Lin and Mei Liu. The brand produces carefully tailored, timeless pieces with family-run Canadian businesses and locally sourced fabrics.

Richmond
Night Market
P.064

Franz Patrick Albana
Owner & designer, 40 decibels

I am an artist who strives to create unconventional garments and accessories for the tribes who do not follow the traditional system of trends. I believe that style conquers trends.

Fresh Roots
Urban Farm Society

Founded by Ilana Labow and led by Mark Schutzbank, Fresh Roots cultivates engaging gardens and programmes that catalyse healthy eating and ecological stewardship in Vancouver.

Granville
Island
P.063

Trout Lake
Farmers
Markets
P.065

25 One of a Few
Map A, P.103

For over a decade, One of a Few has been the spot for fashion-forward customers to find unique and refined items for their wardrobe, from both local and international designers. The boutique is a space for inspiration and sells timeless pieces beyond black and grey, which tends to be the Vancouver-norm. Their selection of footwear and accessories is top-notch for being both distinctive and functional. The store space is relaxing and full of natural light, is accessible from either Water Street or Cordova Street.

🕐 1100–1800 (M–Th & Sa), –1900 (F), 1200–1700 (Su)
🏠 354 Water St., BC V6B 1B2
📞 +1 (604) 605 0685
URL www.oneofafew.com

"A great one stop shop of unique pieces that exemplifies West Coast style. All beautifully made and priced as such."

– Kuh Del Rosario, Elmo's House Artist Residency

26 Atelier St. George
Map B, P.104

An extension of the Kinfolk-style general store named Le Marché St. George, Atelier St. George also features artist and owner Janaki Larsen's own beautiful pottery. The concept space is merchandised exquisitely, delighting the senses with a lovely curation of textiles and housework, clothing and art pieces to promote artisans based in Canada and beyond. The original Le Marché in Riley Park is always bustling with people from the neighbourhood seeking a coffee and tasty bite to eat. It's also a local necessity for grocery staples and ice-cream in summer.

🕐 1100–1800 (Tu–F), –1700 (Sa)
🏠 7 E. 7th Ave., BC V5T 1M4
URL atelierstgeorge.com
🖉 Closed on statutory holidays

"Janaki will often do events on the weekend that showcase local artisan food or other items, and makes and sells her beautiful pottery here!"

– Scott Hawthorn, Native Shoes

27 Antisocial Skateboard Shop
Map B, P.104

On the shortlist for the coolest shops on Main, Antisocial is a Mecca for pavement riders and a key fixture in Vancouver's skate-culture. More than just a shop for decks, trucks, zines, and fabulous kicks, Antisocial also connects skateboarders of different generations with after-hours live music, art shows, record-release parties and video nights. Owner Michelle Pezel is an untiring advocate of this four-wheeled sport herself, and her good effort can be seen outside of the shop, notably at the well-maintained Leeside skatepark and fundraisers for local female skateboarding group Chickflip.

🕐 1100-1800 (M-Sa), 1200-1700 (Su)
🏠 2337 Main St., BC V5T 3C9
📞 +1 (604) 708 5678   URL antisocialshop.com

"Good folks doing good things for the city and the hood. Pick up the much-coveted shop T-shirt. It says Vancouver more than any other souvenir you'll find."
– Andrew Pommier

28 Neighbour

Map A, P.103

Neighbour, a fashion boutique for men and women, boasts exquisitely curated clothing and accessories for those of discerning taste. Located in the popular shopping area Gastown, the store itself is beautifully designed yet can be tricky to find as it is a bit tucked away. So keep your eyes open for the sandwich board outside the Water Street Garage building! Neighbour's selection is refined, as are the staff who are happy to help you with your fashion needs. This is a great place to find a gift for the trendsetter in your life, or to find a unique piece to amp up your wardrobe.

🕐 1100–1900 (M-Sa), 1200–1800 (Su)
🏠 Men: 12 Water St., BCV6B 1A5;
Women: 45 Powell St., BC V6A 1E9
📞 +1 (604) 558 2555, +1 (778) 379 1409
URL www.shopneighbour.com

"Neighbour is in a really great location, so explore the many great shops around. Neighbour Woman just down the street."

– Fahim Kassam

29 The Regional Assembly of Text

Map H, P.107

Started by two art-school friends in 2005, this shop has been offering Vancouver (and Victoria since 2013) beautiful stationery and papery things, alongside small art shows, a typewriter-driven letter-writing club, and artist-made zines and books. Their house line of greeting cards may be found with a corresponding button to wear later. If you love books and/or paper-delights, this is the place for you! A few doors down from Lucky's Comics, and a short walk from Le Marché St. George.

🕐 1100-1800 (M-Sa), 1200-1700 (Su)
🏠 3934 Main St., BC V5V 3P2   📞 +1 (604) 877 2247
🔗 www.assemblyoftext.com
📎 Holiday hours may vary

"Use one of their typewriters and special stationery to bash out a 'foreign correspondent' type letter to someone special."

– Laura Byspalko & Sirish Rao, Indian Summer Festival

30 The Paper Hound

Map A, P.102

With floor to ceiling bookshelves, exposed brick walls, and hidden surprises on every shelf, the stylishly-curated Paper Hound is a magical oasis in a world of disappearing bookstores. Stocked with the best of the new, the old, and the hard-to-find, the care and passion owners Kim Koch and Rod Clarke have for all things print-related is tangible in every inch of this small but fruitful shop. Modelled on the used-book institution MacLeod's up the street, the Paper Hound is a loving update on the vintage bookstore experience of chance discoveries.

🕙 1000–1900 (Su–Th), –2000 (F–Sa)
🏠 344 W. Pender St., BC V6B 1T1
📞 +1 (604) 428 1344
🌐 paperhound.ca

"After you've found some treasure in the shop, take your findings to Finch's across the road or Cartems Donuterie at No.534 to savour them over refreshments."

– Tracy Stefanucci, Vancouver Art/Book Fair

31 Red Cat Records
Map N, P.109

Red Cat Records is a treasure for local music lovers. Owned and operated by artists, it's the spot to pick up new or used albums or cassettes, or concert tickets for your favourite artists. They have recently opened a second location in the Hastings-Sunrise neighbour-hood but their original location on Main Street remains a popular stop. It is a great place to pick up a unique souvenir of Vancouver, like the latest record from local rockers Black Mountain, or let the in-the-know staff help you find something that suits your tastes.

🕓 1100-1900 (M-Th), -2000 (F), 1000-2000 (Sa), -1800 (Su)
🏠 4332 Main St., BC V5V 3P9
📞 +1 (604) 708 9422
URL www.redcat.ca

"Time your visit with one of their many event days, like Record Store Day in April, or Car-Free Day in June."

– Gareth Moses, More Than Human

32 Chinatown
Map A, P.103

Vancouver's Chinatown is one of the city's oldest and most vibrant neighbourhoods. Traces of its former glory can be spotted in the century-old clan association buildings, traditional medicine and tea shops, and classic neon signs. On the front lines of Vancouver's struggle with urban decay, gentrification, and social imbalance, a walk through Chinatown gives a clear picture of the city's past, present, and future. Despite these struggles, locals continue to flock to local institutions such as New Town Bakery for steamed buns, Bamboo Village for unique curios, and Phnom Penh for Cambodian-style fried wings.

🏠 E. Pender St. & Keefer St. near Main St.
URL www.chinatown.today, vancouver-chinatown.com

"Pender, Keefer and Georgia are the best streets to wander. The Youth Collaborative for Chinatown presents a monthly 'Hot & Noisy' mahjong night that's open to all."

– Anna Ling Kaye, Hapa-palooza Festival

33 Welk's General Store
Map H, P.107

Snuggled amongst a brimful of beautiful cafés and designer shops is a longtime neighbourhood staple. A local gift shop, grocery and supply store rolled into one, Welk's has almost everything you need to maintain a healthy lifestyle. From basic home goods to apparels to body care (try Schmidt's Cedarwood + Juniper deodorant), their collections are sourced for obvious reasons – sustainable, moral and safe to use. Drop in to pick up a necessity you forgot to pack or find an inexpensive and practical gift, all while supporting an independently-owned business.

🕐 1000–1800 (M-Sa), 1100– (Su)
🏠 3511 Main St., BC V5V 3N3
📞 +1 (604) 873 3330
URL www.welks.ca

"This is one of my favourite stores around. It truly is like an 'old time' general store. Go in for a look and I'm sure you will find something that you 'need'!"
– Steve Smith-Dla'kwagila

34 Granville Island
Map L, P.109

The keywords at Granville Island are *hand-made*, *cultural*, and *local*. With a large covered public market, critically acclaimed theatres (Arts Club, Improv Centre, Performance Works, Waterfront), an active boatyard, multiple distilleries (sake, beer and gin), and dozens of artisan-owned workshops and craft studios (Net Loft), the attractions of Granville Island are myriad. Live buskers roam the market and the island hosts a number of vibrant cultural festivals. Once a First Nations clamming ground, Granville Island's subsequent industrial past is apparent in the active cement factory on site.

🕐 Public market: 0900-1900 daily
🏠 Granville Island, BC V6H
🔤 granvilleisland.com
🖉 Winter & holiday hours may vary

"The nooks and cranny's of this island has the best eclectic offerings. Check out the floating houses. The architecture is neat and very Vancouver-esque."

– Armin Tehrani & Eunice Quan, Priory

35 Richmond Night Market
Map W, P.111

A tasty and fun place to visit between the months of May and October is the Richmond Night Market, said to be the largest of its kind in North America. Booths offer cute stationery, accessories and novelty items, but it's the food vendors that are most sought after (the Korean-style potato sticks are a favourite). A diverse showcase of live music and dance performances can be seen any night at the market. Free parking lot often fills up before 8pm, so SkyTrain is the way to get there. Take the Canada Line to Bridgeport Station. Seniors and under-tens admit free.

🕒 [Dates for 2017] May 12–Oct 9: 1900–0000 (F–Sa), –2300 (Su & P.H.) 💲 $3.25
🏠 8351 River Rd., BC V6X 1Y4 📞 +1 (604) 244 8448
URL richmondnightmarket.com
🔗 Grab a coupon book at the entrance. Cash only.

"This is where you'll find Vancouver's diverse culture when it comes to food. Bargain if you can!"

– Franz Patrick Albana, 40 decibels

36 Trout Lake Farmers Market
Map J, P.108

Of the many farmers markets in Vancouver, this one is a community favourite, not only for the local treats to be found within, but for the Trout Lake location itself. Pick up a crepe and some fresh fruit and have a picnic in the park! The market is held on Saturdays between May and October, rain or shine, and offers entertainment beyond foodie delights. It's a 15-minute walk from Commercial Drive, where one can continue exploring diverse culinary delicacies offered at the 60 or so restaurants, delis, and shops.

🕐 *[Dates for 2017] May 6–Oct 21: 0900–1400 (Sa)*
🏠 *Lakewood Dr. & E. 13th Ave., BC V5N 4M4*
📞 *+1 (604) 879 3276*
🔗 *eatlocal.org/markets/trout-lake*

"Taste Stein Mountain Farm tomatoes, Harvey's Orchards peaches, and Klippers Organics' apple juice. Definitely indulge yourself in plums from Sapo Bravo!"

– Fresh Roots

Restaurants & Cafés

West Coast fresh, stylish fusion and quality brews

If Vancouver had an unofficial byline, it would be *for foodies, by foodies*. Bestowed with an abundance of blessings including access to the West Coast's freshest ingredients, deeply multicultural influences, and most importantly, rich culinary pickings at a variety of price-points, it is small wonder this is one of the culinary capitals of Canada. For evidence that the global influence goes both ways, consider exhibit A: the hyperlocal 100-mile diet has its origins in Kitsilano.

Vegetarians and vegans will delight in the creative interpretations of local and sustainable harvest bounty, while seafood-lovers will near nirvana when sampling B.C.'s fantastic wild salmon, velvety sablefish, and during a few fleeting weeks (late spring), the incredible spot prawn. The innovations of local food trucks and authentic ethnic eateries (read: dosas, dumplings, poke, tacos, pho, ramen, sushi) will provide endless budget delights, while those ready to splurge will revel in the fine dining options, be it nose-to-tail haute cuisine, authentic Japanese, or a hybrid of both (or any other two cuisines). Serious tea and coffee lovers will find sophisticated caffeine-meccas aplenty, and there's world-class gourmet ice cream, gelato, and chocolate to be discovered as well.

Craig Stanghetta
Founder & principal, Ste. Marie

I love to travel, arguably this is why I love the work we do. We love this place as it allows us to have a lifestyle seldom afforded designers and artists, such as trekking, crabbing and sailing.

Ask for Luigi
P.072

Martin Nielsen
Principal, DIALOG

Martin Nielsen has over two decades of experience in design practice. He is passionate about developing socially, economically, and environmentally responsible design solutions.

Jasper Sloan Yip
Singer-songwriter

I have been performing, touring, and recording with my experimental folk-rock band since 2010. We released two LPs in 2010 and 2013. The third named Post Meridiem comes in 2017.

Osteria
Savio Volpe
P.070

Aubade
Coffee
P.073

Dylan Rekert
Art Director, Kit and Ace

Dylan Rekert joined apparel brand Kit and Ace as Graphic Design Manager in 2014. He's also a partner in spin club Ride Cycle Club, along with J.J. Wilson.

The Acorn
P.075

Meeru Dhalwala
Chef & co-owner, Vij's & Rangoli

I'm also a cookbook author and founder of Joy of Feeding at UBC Farm, an annual international food festival and fundraiser for the Farm's sustainable agriculture programme.

Jay Dodge & Sherry Yoon
Boca del Lupo

With the pair at helm, as producer and art director, Boca del Lupo's focus is on designs and plays. Their presentations also include Micro Performance Series and MediaLab.

Liberty
Bakery
P.074

Vij's
P.076

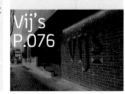

Ken Tsui
Co-founder, Here There

Here There creates experiences to activate brands. Ken Tsui lives each day like it's his last, busy giving away prized possessions and apologetically scrambling to get them back night and day.

Yuji's from Japan
P.078

David Hawksworth
Hawksworth Restaurant

Chef David Hawksworth realised his culinary dream in 2011 when he opened Hawksworth Restaurant and Bel Cafe to critical acclaim. He's also the Chef Ambassador for Air Canada.

Alex Yu
Fashion designer

I create luxury streetwear that ponders the very definition of femininity in a modern, quirky way. My aesthetics rollick the happy emotions of childhood, nostalgia and wanderlust.

Dynasty Seafood Restaurant
P.077

Kingyo Izakaya
P.079

David Khang
Artist & art educator

I have practiced dentistry for 25 years, art for 15, and taught at ECUAD for 10. But that formula is about to change, as I am now pursuing a law programme at UBC.

Six Acres
P.082

Trevor Brady
Photographer & director

I love minimalist designs and fine magazines like *Dansk*. Don't hate me for loving New Times Roman Italic and Helvetica Neue. Cape Town is my birth place and Berlin is my favourite city.

Sarah Tesla
Founder, Make

Sarah Tesla also writes for *Lost Not Found*. When she is not running her digital agency Make, she can be found tromping through East Africa or exploring B.C. on her motorbike.

Wildebeest
P.080

Bistro Wagon Rouge
P.083

37 Osteria Savio Volpe
Map D, P.105

Since its opening in 2015, Savio Volpe has earned a strong reputation for its rustic-chic Italian-style fare. A self-directed project between Ste. Marie studio principal Craig Stanghetta, restaurateur Paul Grunberg and chef Mark Perrier, this charming fox hole delivers simple but delicate flavours of handmade fresh pastas and wood-grilled farm-fresh produce the traditional osteria way, alongside an all Italian wine list. Great place to visit seven days a week for early dinner or spritz and salumi all the way through to full family meals. Reservations recommended.

🕐 1900–2230 daily
🏠 615 Kingsway, BC V5T 3K5
📞 +1 (604) 428 0072
URL www.saviovolpe.com

"Design, food and conviviality are the driving forces and they exist harmoniously here. This is one of our studio's favourite designs being such a personal project."

– Craig Stanghetta, Ste. Marie

38 Ask for Luigi
Map A, P.103

Tucked away in an adorable East Vancouver building, Ask for Luigi's 70's style casual chic is paired with the major kitchen talent of chef-owner Jean-Christophe Poirier. Hand-rolled pasta is the star attraction: try to go with friends so you can sample a full spectrum of the flavour-explosions available. Brunch, lunch and dinner are all excellent but Luigi's is notorious for lines. Luckily there are great watering holes and interesting shops in the surrounding neighbourhood to peruse while you wait.

🕐 Brunch/Lunch: 0900-1430 (Sa-Su), 1130- (Tu-F), Dinner: 1730-2230 (Tu-Th), -2300 (F-Sa), -2130 (Su)
🏠 305 Alexander St., BC V6A 1C4
📞 +1 (604) 428 2544
URL www.askforluigi.com

"Check out the busy shipping/container port at the waterfront and visit the Inform furniture showroom on Railway Street while you are there."

– Martin Nielsen, DIALOG

39 Aubade Coffee

Map A, P.103

Coffee fanatics will find a kindred spirit in Aubade proprietor-barista Eldric Kuzma. The focus is on the smoothest cup of filter coffee possible, pursued with obsessively-curated beans and a specialised variety of coffee-processing gadgets. With the simplest of menus (coffee, tea, pastries), Eldric's coffee counter is the front half of the curio-rich vintage store Space Lab (there's a barber shop in the back). On Mondays, coffee hounds will have to slake their shakes elsewhere.

🕐 0800–1500 (Tu), –1600 (W–F), 0900–1600 (Sa–Su)
🏠 230 E. Pender St., BC V6A 1T3
📞 +1 (604) 219 9247
URL aubadecoffee.info

"Spacelab is perhaps the city's coolest shop for antiques and oddities, so this is kind of a two-for-one. Grab a coffee from Eldric and browse the wares."

– Jasper Sloan Yip

40 Liberty Bakery
Map H, P.107

A place of whimsy and elegance, the homey charm of Liberty Bakery is in the details: rustic ceramic mugs for the coffee, knitted cosies on the tea pots, and tastefully arranged classic portraits on the white-painted wood walls. Owned by three Vancouver artists who decided to save a popular neighbourhood café, Liberty retains the original bakery's Nordic roots with fresh and local ingredients. The Totoro-shaped gingerbread cookies are irresistible, and the croissants are top-notch. Decisions, decisions!

🕐 0800–1800 (M–F), 0900– (Sa–Su)
🏠 3699 Main St., BC V5V
📞 +1 (604) 709 9999
URL www.liberty-bakery.com

"One of the owners is Rodney Graham who I admire. Its easy, laid back vibe is perfect for a Sunday Morning when I'm in need of a little inspiration."

– Dylan Rekert, Kit and Ace

41 The Acorn
Map H, P.107

Modern "vegetable-forward" restaurant caters to locals who demand creative and elegant meat-free cuisine, and is coveted by veg and non-veg eaters alike. The dining room is cosy, and as this is a popular spot and tables are given on a first-come-first-served basis, there is usually a line-up. The Caesar Salad dressing is made without the anchovies but still has the umami punch. Try their signature cocktails with dinner (also a great list of creative non-alcoholic bevies), or pop by for their happy hour at the end of the day. They are also open weekends for brunch.

🕐 1730-2200 (Su-Th), -2300 (F-Sa),
Weekend brunch: 1000-1430
🏠 3995 Main St., BC V5V 3P3 📞 +1 (604) 566 9001
🔗 www.theacornrestaurant.ca

"Go for its cool and funky ambience and delicious, original vegetarian cuisine. This place is a local favourite so tourists will be dining with a Vancouver flair."

– Meeru Dhalwala, Vij's & Rangoli

42 Vij's
Map M, P.109

When people speak of Vij's, they lapse into superlatives: best Indian food in North America, the funkiest, the most creative, and downright delicious. Behind the rich copper detail of the elegant dining room and the stylish patrons sipping decadent cocktails is the grounded and astute sensibility of owners Vikram Vij and Meeru Dhalwala (P.068) to employ an all-female kitchen staff and to use fresh, local and sustainable ingredients. For all the flavour minus the wait, try their equally excellent bistro, Rangoli on West 11th Avenue.

🕐 1730 till late daily
🏠 3106 Cambie St., BC V5Z 2W2
📞 +1 (604) 736 6664
URL www.vijsrestaurant.ca
🎟 Walk-ins only

"Go early if you want a seat right away or later to avoid the wait. Or put your name on the wait list and walk around the neighbourhood."

– Jay Dodge & Sherry Yoon, Boca del Lupo

43 Dynasty Seafood Restaurant
Map T, P.110

Some say Vancouver's Cantonese food rivals the best in Asia, and the chandeliered Dynasty Seafood is a fine candidate to prove such claims. Dim sum line-ups are legendary even with reservations, but worthwhile for the reward of plump, juicy dumplings and buttery pastries. Dinner service is a revelation, with many authentic and unusual dishes on the menu, as well as the impressive parade of giant king crab and grouper platters that will be swirling past en route to other tables.

- ⏱ 1000–1500, 1700–2230 daily
- 🏠 108–777 W. Broadway, BC V5Z 4J7
- ☎ +1 (604) 876 8388
- URL www.dynasty-restaurant.ca
- 🖉 Complimentary parking available

"Their menu is approachable for a novice and tasty enough to keep the seasoned diners coming back time and time again. Order lots. The more the merrier."

– Ken Tsui, Here There

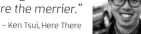

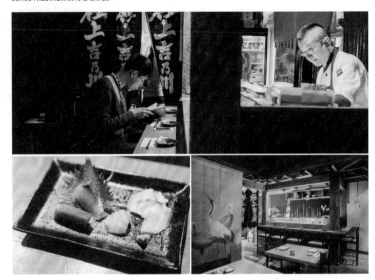

44 Yuji's from Japan
Map X, P.111

Humble and charming, this intimate restaurant is named for its chef-proprietor Yuji Otsuka, who can be seen most nights behind the sushi counter cracking jokes with new customers and regulars alike. For a full sampling of Yuji's meticulously crafted dishes, treat yourself to the delectable surprises of the extremely well-priced omakase menus. If not, make sure to mine the "specialties" menu for treasures like the cornflake-crusted prawn tempura. Only open for dinner. Book ahead to avoid disappointment on weekends.

🕐 1700 till late (M–Sa except P.H.)
🏠 2083 Alma St., BC V6R 4N6
📞 +1 (604) 428 4688
URL www.yujis.ca

"The fish is fresh and the dishes are authentic. Must try watercress gomae. Have a stroll along West 4th Ave for some shopping before dinner."

– David Hawksworth, Hawksworth Restaurant

45 Kingyo Izakaya
Map E, P.106

A harmonious blend of quirky and cool, this lively, upbeat izakaya joint is a cut above the already top-notch contemporary Japanese dining offerings in town. With fantastic décor that's part Asian zen, part re-imagined nostalgia, each Kingyo dish is a delicate revelation, and the drinks are plentiful, tasty, and occasionally presented in ogre-shaped hand-built ceramics. If you like it here, make sure to try the other Tamaru Shoten restaurants in town (Suika, Rajio, and Raisu), all delicious, no two alike.

🕐 1130–1430, 1730–2330 (Su-Th), –0000 (F-Sa)
🏠 871 Denman St., BC V6G 2L9
📞 +1 (604) 608 1677
URL www.kingyo-izakaya.ca

"*The best part here is lunch. Their limited edition bento box that comprises more than 12 of their popular dishes sell out within the first ten minutes.*"

– Alex Yu

46 Wildebeest

Map A, P.103

Protein lovers will delight in this hoof-to-tail haven with emphasis on locavore and slow food cooking paired with excellent libations. Not to be missed is the multi-textured sous-vide egg garnished with popcorn grits and crispy chicken skin. The exposed brick dining room features communal harvest tables and intimate booths under dangling Edison bulbs. Pop across the street to the redeveloped historical Woodward's Building after to shoot hoops or admire the giant Stan Douglas photo mural recreation of a 1971 riot.

🕐 1700 till late (M-F), 1000-1400, 1700 till late (Sa-Su)
🏠 120 W. Hastings St., BC V6B 1G8
📞 +1 (604) 687 6880
URL wildebeest.ca

"Frankly, because you don't go home hungry after dropping $$$ at pretender tapas places. That leaves Wildebeest, Chambar and La Quercia in a three-way tie."

– David Khang

47 Six Acres
Map A, P.103

Sneak a break from your Gastown shopping to grab a tasty bite and something to sip at Six Acres. Known for great prices and its 40-some varieties of craft beers, the blissfully quaint pub also boasts the right amount of brick and quirk, plantlife and good music that draw locals to chill out or meet for a catch up. Six Acres' extra long happy hours, which run from the time doors open to 6pm, mean anytime is a good time to binge on beers without dropping too much money. On those rare non-rainy days, ask for a serving of frites out on the outdoor patio to celebrate the precipitation-break!

🕐 1130–2330 (Su-Th), –0030 (F-Sa)
🏠 203 Carrall St., BC V6B 2J2
📞 +1 (604) 488 0110 URL sixacres.ca
🔗 Weekend happy hours might change after brunch menu launch.

"*Get the Czechvar beer, big bottle, my fav. Love the salt pepper wings, and beet salad.*"

– Trevor Brady

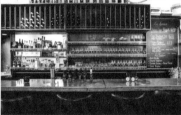

48 Bistro Wagon Rouge

Map I, P.108

Those looking for a French-food-fix will be happy to stumble on Bistro Wagon Rouge, which is off the beaten path. This unassuming, unpretentious bistro in East Vancouver is a culinary wonderland, paired beautifully with down-to-earth, high-end service. There's always something new in menu, and its diverse offerings will inspire you to order several dishes to share. Walk-ins only, so get there early or be prepared for a wait. But if the wait is long, grab a beer at Parallel 49th Brewing on Triumph Street, or at Doan's Craft Brewing across the road.

🕐 1700–2200 (Tu–Sa)
🏠 1869 Powell St., BCV5L 1H9
📞 +1 (604) 251 4070
🔗 bistrowagonrouge.com

"Grab a seat at the bar. Watch your cheese plate or butter lettuce salad being prepared, while you sip your Kir Royale and catch-up on the day with the bartender."

– Sarah Tesla, Make

Kissa Tanto, P.097

Nightlife

Local breweries, cinema-chic lounges and neighbourhood dives

Vancouver's nightlife offers something for everyone's tastes: arteries of local breweries, dance clubs, casinos, hard rock bars, 24-hour vegan eats, tiki time, carefully-crafted cocktails, lovingly-crafted artisanal desserts, and with over one thousand bands based in town, live music aplenty. *The Georgia Straight* is the best directory of weekly listings.

While the bold and adventurous will find diversion on the neon-bejewelled Granville strip, infamous for attracting the freshly-turned-nineteen market from the surrounding lower Mainland, there are many pockets of great nightlife tucked away throughout the city. Nearby Gastown and Yaletown cater to slightly older and better-heeled crowds, with the former excelling at designer cocktails, Irish pubs, and stylish eats, the latter skewing on the oyster and wine bar side of things. Near Stanley Park is the West End, whose late night gay bars and dance clubs such as the venerable Celebrities (*celebritiesnightclub.com*) promise legendary fun for all. Quieter Kitsilano is home to many a hidden gem and the occasional jazz club. For the craft-brew aficionado, Main Street and Commercial Drive provides an endless parade of unique watering-holes.

Alex Nelson & Beau House
Partners, Post Projects

Post Projects is a branding and design agency working for small, medium and large organisations across a diverse range of platforms and disciplines.

The Biltmore Cabaret
P.090

Tariq Hussain
Writer & singer-songwriter

Besides his solo recordings, Tariq Hussain also records with Brasstronaut. He's writing a memoir about the challenges of growing up as a first generation Canadian kid with musical dreams.

Leanne Dunic
Writer, musician & artist

Leanne Dunic is the artistic director of the Powell Street Festival, the author of *To Love the Coming End*, and the singer-guitarist of The Deep Cove. She co-produced CITIx60 Vancouver.

Fortune Sound Club
P.088

Jackalope's Neighbourhood Dive
P.091

Crackle Crème
P.093

Tetsuro Shigematsu
Writer, performer & scholar

I create autobiographical spectacles that combine theatre performance and live cinema. My shows are produced by Vancouver Asian Canadian Theatre.

Tomoyo Ihaya
Artist

I came here as an art student in 1996 and stayed on. While making art, I engage with different techniques and combine my creative process with travel and living in places such as India.

Lindsey Hampton
Ceramicist & graphic designer

Lindsey Hampton is a multidisciplinary artist, focusing on print and ceramics, both functional and sculptural. She also adapts her vision to other mediums, such as photography and music.

The NAAM
P.092

33 Acres Brewing Co.
P.094

Grady Mitchell
Photographer & writer

I fell in love with photography and writing because they let me meet and learn about people I otherwise wouldn't. I've shot photos and write for clients, both commercial and editorial.

The Lido
P.096

Glasfurd & Walker
Design studio

Phoebe Glasfurd and Aren Field-walker form Glasfurd & Walker. Their folio includes branding and identity, packaging, web, marketing collateral and signage design.

LACAR
Jewellery label

Morgan Carrier and Shira Laye started LACAR in 2013. Their jewellery is equally influenced by the past and present, gathering design ideas from travel and observed artefacts.

The Boxcar
P.095

Kissa Tanto
P.097

Paul Wong
Artist

Writing, publishing and teaching have been an important part of Paul Wong's praxis. With a career spanning four decades, the media-maestro is an instrumental proponent to contemporary art.

Guilt & Co.
P.099

Tomasz Wagner
Photographer

Photographer and cinematographer Tomasz Wagner blends art and photojournalism while documenting weddings at home in Vancouver and worldwide.

Katie So
Illustrator & tattooer

After graduating from graphic design school, Katie So found her place in small press comics. From there, she honed her skills creating brush and ink work, a style that recurs in her tattoo art.

The Fox
Cabaret
P.098

Here There
P.100

49 Fortune Sound Club
Map A, P.103

Fortune covers the full spectrum of sound from Wed to Sun. If you appreciate sub-bass and just the right amount of treble this is the club for you. What was once the infamous Ming's Chinese Restaurant is now a revamped space focusing on innovative design, art that can't be messed with, and eco-friendly features – all of which are brought to life by the most official Funktion One sound system. Wander around to make sure you find all the rooms and artist installations throughout the building. Try to make it to Happy Endings Fridays, a flagship event since 2010, to see how Vancouver ends their workweek.

⏱ Hours & price vary with events
🏠 147 E. Pender St., BC V6A 1T5
📞 +1 (604) 569 1758
URL fortunesoundclub.com
🎟 19+

"See you on the dance floor."

– Alex Nelson & Beau House, Post Projects

50 The Biltmore Cabaret
Map B, P.104

The Biltmore Cabaret holds a special place in the hearts of Vancouverites, particularly those who are serious about music. Over the years, the intimate stage of the Biltmore Cabaret puts on a diverse programme of live shows by the likes of Warpaint, Jonathan Richmond and Thurston Moore. From burlesque to DJ nights to local bands and touring acts, this eclectic space has heard it all. A big queue emerges around midnight. Check out the vintage game machines at the back while the bands are warming up if you aren't keen to be right up front.

🕐 Showtimes & prices vary with shows
🏠 2755 Prince Edward St., BC V5T 0A9
📞 +1 (604) 676 0541 URL biltmorecabaret.com
🔗 19+, with photo ID

"There's something about the atmosphere of this venue that works for me, probably because of the real music lover's kinda crowd."
– Tariq Hussain

51 Jackalope's Neighbourhood Dive

Map I, P.108

This unassuming eatery and bar is close to Red Cat Records (#31) for those wanting to pick up some records before digging into some rock 'n' roll and seriously good eats. Listen to an album by Genesis while having a drink next to a seductive photo of The Boss. Be sure to share the half-order of vegetarian nachos (reiterating: share). Meat-eaters should definitely try the honey-garlic chicken wings. Ask the staff to tell you about 'Neüterhead/Ace of Spays'. Jackalope's opens early and serves legendary brunch until 2pm on weekends.

🕐 1500-2300 (M-Th), 1000-0000 (F-Sa), 1000- (Su)
🏠 2257 E. Hastings St., BC V5L 1V3
📞 +1 (604) 568 6674 🌐 jackalopesdive.com

"A visit to the bathroom is a must (pet-lovers are in for a treat!)"

– Leanne Dunic

52 The NAAM
Map K, P.109

On the one hand a cosy fifty-year-old vegetarian restaurant isn't a typical nightlife mainstay, on the other hand, it is so very Vancouver that it is. Warm and homey, with an emphasis on organic and sustainable comfort food, the 24/7 NAAM had its salad days in the 60s, back when Fourth Avenue was still called Rainbow Road. This Kitsilano spot starts serving breakfast at 6am, which runs until 11.30am on weekdays, and 1pm through the weekend. The wooden walls are decked in rotating exhibits of colourful local art, and every evening sees live music from 7-10pm.

🕐 *24 hrs except Dec 25*
🏠 *2724 W. 4th Ave., BC V6K 1R1*
📞 *+1 (604) 738 7151*
🔗 *www.thenaam.com*

"This is a funky vegetarian restaurant with food yummy enough for omnivores, plus they have a garden patio, and staff that are genuinely hipster yet friendly."

– Tetsuro Shigematsu

53 Crackle Crème

Map A, P.103

If drinks and dancing aren't your evening jam, take a stroll on Vancouver's sweeter side at Crackle Crème. Serving up artisanal crème brûlée (try the black sesame), made-to-order caramelised Belgian liege waffles, and ridiculously adorable macaroons, this tiny dessert café is owner Daniel Wang's homage to the delicious things in life, and a refuge from his former work as an automotive painter. Located on the edge of Chinatown, this stretch of Union Street also has a fine assortment of eateries, bars, and a mix of fashion-forward and traditional Chinese shops.

🕐 1500–2200 (M–F), 1400– (Sa) 1400–2100 (Su)
🏠 245 Union St., BC V6A 4C3
☎ +1 (778) 847 8533
URL www.cracklecreme.com

"Daniel's crème brûlées are all so tasty, with flavours like lavender, earl grey and salted caramel. Now this place is 'hot' so expect a line-up on the weekend."

– Tomoyo Ihaya

 54 **33 Acres Brewing Co.**
Map B, P.104

Don't let the name fool you. This family-owned and operated micro-brewery is more than just impressive house brews. Open at 9am, the bright, minimalist space is a great choice to grab a waffle-brunch at weekends or hearty grubs during the week, served up to 2pm. 33 Acres' seasonals are what keep their loyal fans returning, available for fills, bottles or on draft. 33 Acres occasionally does collaborations with local food trucks on location as well. So expect delicious comfort food such as tacos, yummy pizzas or Korean grills for lunch or dinner from time to time.

🕐 0900-2300 (M-F), 1000- (Sa-Su & P.H.)
🏠 15 W. 8th Ave., BC V5Y 1M8
📞 +1 (604) 620 4589
URL 33acresbrewing.com

"I prefer to go in the morning as it tends to get really busy later on but if that's your thing, the beer is great too."
– Lindsey Hampton

55 The Boxcar
Map A, P.103

Be mindful of the address, as this little no-sign
bar can be hard to find. Slotted into the narrow
space between a legendary club and sister
space, The Cobalt, and Pizzeria Farina, this spot
is especially enjoyable on the warmer days
when they open the space up to give it a cool
patio-vibe. Happy hour is between 5-7pm. Stop
by in the early evening to sample exceptional
local craft beers on 24 taps before the crowds
arrive. If your looking to get hectic then mi-
grate next door. The Cobalt is a fantastic place
to catch live music, karaoke, or a drag show.

🕐 1700-0100 (M-Th), 1600-0200 (F-Sa), 1600- (Su)
🏠 917 Main St., BC V6A 2V8
📞 +1 (604) 398 4010   📘 TheBoxcarVancouver
🔗 thecobalt.ca/the-boxcar

"*Great beer selection and the back patio is bumping
in the summer. You can order Vancouver's best pizza
from Farina and bring it into the bar.*"

– Grady Mitchell

56 The Lido
Map B, P.105

Casual bar vibes meet hipster house party at this cosy neighbourhood bar just off Main Street. Once a namesake grocery store that young neighbours never see open, The Lido offers a small stage for intimate live shows and a homely vibe where locals can mingle with friendly strangers over well-priced drinks on a plush vintage couch. There isn't much in the way of food here, so make sure you eat before you come. Check out their event calendar for a surprise hit. The shows are always free, and the quality is excellent.

🕐 1600–0100 (M–Th), 1400–0200 (F–Sa), 1400–0100 (Su)
🏠 518 E. Broadway, BC V5T 1X4
📞 +1 (604) 879 5436
f The Lido
🔗 Cash only

"Cap off a day of exploring the Mount Pleasant neighbourhood by taking in some music and some cocktails at this local hangout."

– Morgan Carrier & Shira Laye, LACAR

57 Kissa Tanto
Map A, P.103

Ascend a dark staircase off a Chinatown lane and enter an intimate jazz lounge with 1960s glamour and intrigue. Described by designer Craig Stanghetta (P.068) as a nod to Tokyo's Hotel Okura and a wink to architect Gio Ponti, locals know Kissa Tanto as one of the classiest places in town for seductive cocktails and innovative Japanese-Italian high cuisine. Brought by the power team of Tannis Ling and chef Joel Watanabe (Corsican-Japanese himself), this is sister restaurant to the amazing Bao Bei Brasserie, also nearby and worthy of pilgrimage.

🕐 1730–0000 (Tu–Sa)
🏠 263 E. Pender St., BC V6A 1T8
📞 +1 (778) 379 8078 URL www.kissatanto.com
🔗 Reservations recommended for parties of 4 or more

"Sexiest bar in town. Order the Irish Coffee or Espresso Martini. A cheesey classic that they do perfectly."

– Glasfurd & Walker

58 The Fox Cabaret
Map B, P.104

A former porn-theatre reborn as a premier venue for live music, dancing, film screenings, The Fox Cabaret draws a rowdy crowd every day of the week. Upstairs is a tiki David Lynch dreamscape converted from an actual projection booth with a sparkly bar and an eclectic musical range. Catch obscure and eclectic space rock, post-punk, synth-pop, and afrobeat on a Sunday night when Darwin Meyers spins the vinyl. The Fox is in a brewery district, so consider hitting one of the top craft breweries before or after a visit to the Fox. Brassneck Brewery and Main Street Brewing are just steps away.

🕐 2000-0100 (Su-Th), -0200 (F-Sa)
🏠 2321 Main St., BC V5T 3C9
✉ info@foxcabaret.com
f @FoxCabaret, @foxprojectionroom
URL foxcabaret.com 🔗 19+

"If you want to get down and off grid, check out late night techno music pansexual events. Best to follow on Facebook."

– Paul Wong

59 Guilt & Co.
Map A, P.103

A city-centre hotspot for live performances, this basement bar transports you to whatever era the band is playing. Swing, jazz, soul with lots of modern covers mixed in every single night, Guilt & Co. is always packed to the brim, especially on Fridays and Saturdays. With low-lighting and an underground speakeasy vibe, it is an ideal spot to try an inventive cocktail and play a board game after a day of exploring the city. Look for a sandwich board outside Chill Winston on Gassy Jack Square as it's easy to miss.

🕐 2000 till late daily
🏠 1 Alexander St., BC V6A 1B2
URL www.guiltandcompany.com

"It's dang classy. I don't dance. But you should."
– Katie So

60 Here There

Lizzy Karp and Ken Tsui (P.069) who founded and run studio Here There are behind some of the most fun and exciting events happening in Vancouver. The twosome thinks beyond disciplines, regular venues, and the conventional, and seeks to engage people with places in a compelling and memorable way. Vancouver owes Here There for their role in bringing Vancouverites together via pop-up meals, dumpling festivals, live music, and more. Be sure to attend one of their events if you can! You may even meet someone to be your Vancouver pen pal.

🕐🏠 *Hours & location vary with events*
🌐 hello@heretherestudio.com
URL www.heretherestudio.com

"Ken and Lizzy's pop-up multi-sensory events are unique, fun, and unexpected. They happen sporadically so get on their mailing list to be in the know."
– Tomasz Wagner

MAP A

Bussard Station

Royal Dinette

RBC Royal Bank

Waterfront

W CORDOVA

W PENDER ST

DUNSMUIR ST

HOMER ST

W GEORGIA ST

Bill Reid Gallery

W HASTINGS ST

SEYMOUR ST

La Taqueria Pinche Taco Shop

ROBSON ST

HORNBY ST

22

Granville

30

5

Robson Square

Vancouver City Centre

HOMER ST

Field & Social

DUNSMUIR ST

GRANVILLE ST

SEYMOUR ST

Commodore Ballroom

Medina

W GEORGIA ST

CAMBIE ST

The Orpheum

20

HOMER ST

The Roxy

RUTS Wednesdays, LED bar @Caprice Nightclub

The Buzz Cafe & Espresso Bar

Contemporary Art Gallery

Homer St Cafe and Bar

HELMCKEN ST

CAMBIE ST

HOMER ST

BC Place

DISTRICT MAP : **MOUNT PLEASANT**

MAP B

Beta5 Chocolates

14

W 1ST AVE

E 2ND AVE

Earnest Ice Cream

Faculty Brewing Co.

Winsor Gallery Corporation

Catriona Jeffries

E 2ND AVE

Chernoff Fine Art + Framing

Macaulay & Co. Fine Art

Gallery 295

E 4TH AVE

R&B Ale & Pizza House

grunt gallery

Brassneck Brewery

26

W 7TH AVE

58

27

Main Street Brewing Co.

54

Guelph Park

Budgies Burritos

FIELD Contemporary

W BROADWAY

BAF Gallery

Sunny Spot Cafe

MAIN ST

PRINCE EDWARD ST

E 11TH AVE

50

MAP H

....

- 14_The Flats
- 26_Atelier St. George
- 27_Antisocial Skateboard Shop
- 50_The Biltmore Cabaret
- 54_33 Acres Brewing Co.
- 58_The Fox Cabaret

MAP C

PRINCESS AVE

MakerLabs ●

Burning Hearts
Soul Club @ Astoria ●

13 E HASTINGS ST

● Wil Aballe Art Projects

E PENDER ST

KEEFER ST

1000 ft.

Monte Clark Gallery ●
Equinox Gallery ●

GREAT NORTHERN WAY

MAP D

ST GEORGE ST

FRASER ST

E 14TH AVE

37 **16**

KINGSWAY ● Les Faux
Bourgeois

The Black
Lodge ●

56

ST GEORGE ST

E BROADWAY

ST GEORGE ST

FRASER ST

MAP D
▼

1000 ft.

1000 ft.

- 1_Sylvia Hotel
- 18_Chan Centre for the Performing Arts
- 23_Museum of Anthropology
- 45_Kingyo Izakaya

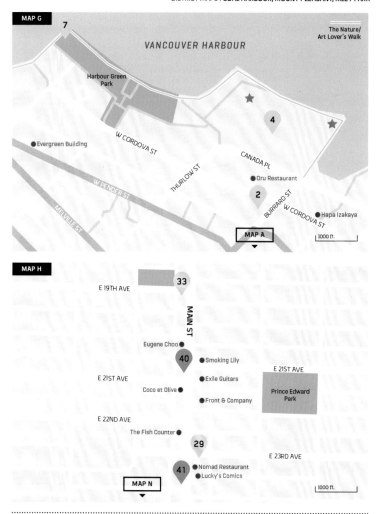

- 2_Marine Building
- 4_Vancouver Convention Centre West
- 7_LightShed
- 29_The Regional Assembly of Text
- 33_Welk's General Store
- 40_Liberty Bakery
- 41_The Acorn

MAP I

48

POWELL ST

Doan's Craft
Brewing Company

Parallel 49
Brewing Co

DUNDAS ST

VICTORIA DR

SEMLIN DR

LAKEWOOD DR

TEMPLETON DR

FRANKLIN ST

51

E HASTINGS ST

1000 ft.

MAP J

19

Commercial-Broadway

E BROADWAY

COMMERCIAL DR

LAKEWOOD DR

Bandidas Taqueria

E 13TH AVE

E 13TH AVE

36

1000 ft.

- 19_The Rio Theatre
- 36_Trout Lake Farmers Markets
- 48_Bistro Wagon Rouge
- 51_Jackalope's Neighbourhood Dive

- 31_Red Cat Records
- 34_Granville Island
- 42_Vij's
- 52_The NAAM

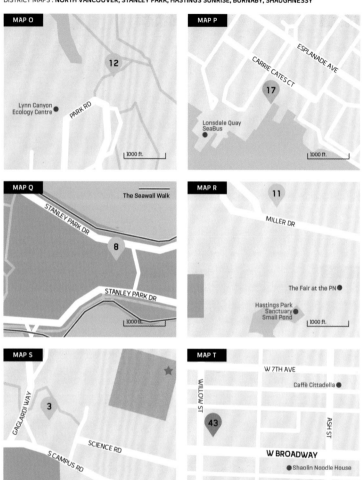

- 3_Simon Fraser University
- 8_The Totem Poles @Stanley Park
- 11_Hastings Racecourse
- 12_Lynn Canyon
- 17_Presentation House Gallery (The Polygon Gallery)
- 43_Dynasty Seafood Restaurant

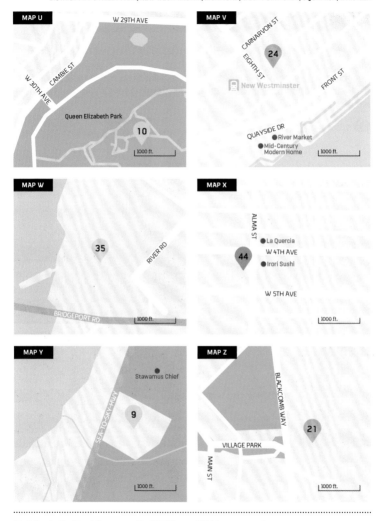

- 9_Sea to Sky Gondola
- 10_Bloedel Conservatory
- 21_Audain Art Museum
- 24_New Media Gallery
- 35_Richmond Night Market
- 44_Yuji's from Japan
- ★ Public artwork

Accommodation

Hip hostels, fully-equipped apartments & swanky hotels

No journey is perfect without a good night's sleep to recharge. Whether you're backpacking or on a business trip, our picks combine top quality and convenience, whatever your budget.

$ < $120   **$** $121–200   **$** $201+

Rosewood Hotel Georgia

Recently updated, this hotel captures the best of 1920s grandeur in every part. The Garden Terrace is an unmissable stop, as well as Hawksworth and Prohibition if you want to continue living it up at the hotel. Hawksworth is a great place to unwind over a cocktail and talk about the art you just saw at the opposite Vancouver Art Gallery. Wellness facilities include spa treatment, gym and an indoor saltwater lap pool.

🏠 801 W. Georgia St., BC V6C 1P7
📞 +1 (604) 682 5566
URL rosewoodhotels.com

LEVEL Vancouver

From 46-sqm studios to 110-sqm sleeping two to four plus kids, LEVEL apartments are fully equipped to make you feel at home. All suites feature a full-size kitchen with an oven and dishwasher, as well as washer/dryer and free access to gym facilities and heated outdoor pool. LEVEL is pet-friendly. The area abounds in top diners, galleries and nightclubs.

 1022 Seymour St., BC V6B 0G1
 +1 (604) 685 3835 stayinglevel.com

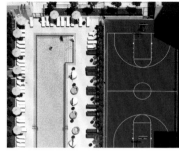

The Burrard

Calling themselves "the perfect city base camp", The Burrard exudes retro-modern character from every joist and sightline. Recent revamp combines its 1950s motor inn aesthetics and neat facilities, adding a lush courtyard for outdoor lounging and some ping pong fun. The 3-star hotel also offers free Brodie cruiser bike rentals. Some rooms welcome dogs.

🏠 1100 Burrard St., BC V6Z 1Y7
📞 +1 (604) 681 2331 URL theburrard.com

St. Regis Hotel Vancouver

🏠 602 Dunsmuir St., BC V6B 1Y6
☎ +1 (604) 681 1135
URL www.stregishotel.com

Granville Island Hotel

🏠 1253 Johnston St., BC V6H 3R9
☎ +1 (800) 663 1840
URL granvilleislandhotel.com

Notes

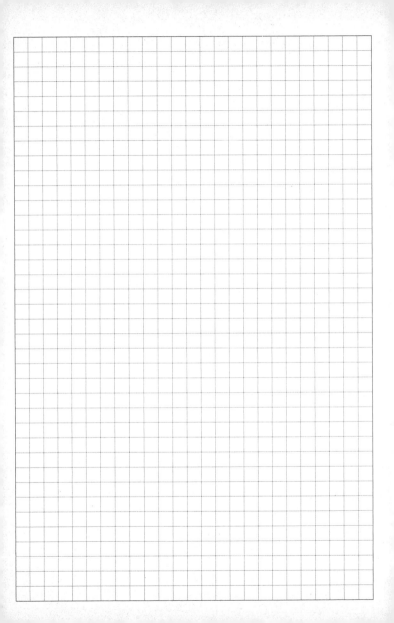

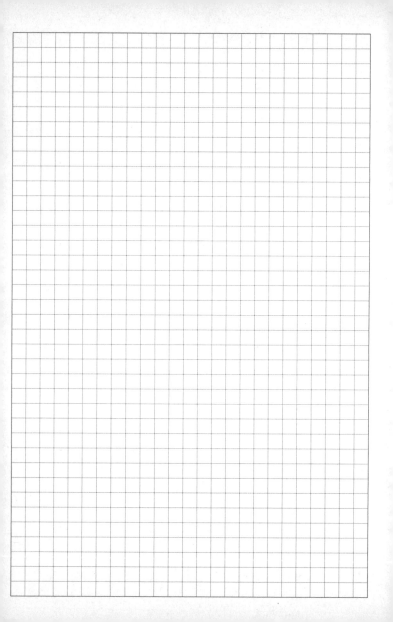

Index

**Alvin Kwan & Vince Lo
@Studio Faculty,** *P.023–025*
studiofaculty.com

**Courtenay Webber
@The Future,** *P.042*
the-future.ca

David Arias, *P.038*
arias.ca,
davidarias.vsco.co,
@ariasdavid

Dylan Staniul @Burnkit, *P.045*
www.burnkit.com

Glasfurd & Walker, *P.097*
www.glasfurdandwalker.com

Lindsey Hampton, *P.094*
www.lindseyhampton.com

Music

David Phu, *P.048–049*
vimeo.com/davidphu

**Gareth Moses @More Than
Human,** *P.060*
morethanhumanrecords.com

Jasper Sloan Yip, *P.073*
jaspersloanyip.com

Tariq Hussain, *P.090*
www.tariqmusiq.com,
www.brasstronaut.com

Performing arts

**Jay Dodge & Sherry Yoon
@Boca del Lupo,** *P.076*
bocadellupo.com

Tetsuro Shigematsu, *P.092*
shiggy.com
Portrait by Mika Shigematsu

Publishing

**Jeff Khonsary @New
Documents,** *P.016–017*
new-documents.org

Jordan Abel, *P.022*
www.jordanabel.ca

**Meagan Albrechtson
@Lolita,** *P.046–047*
lolita-magazine.com

Suzanne Ma, *P.020*
www.suzannema.com

Photo & other credits

Ask for Luigi, *P.072*
(All) Ask for Luigi

Audain Art Museum, *P.044*
(All) Audain Art Museum

Bistro Wagon Rouge, *P.083*
*(Right bottom & food) Claudette
Carracedo*

**Chan Centre for the
Performing Arts,** *P.040–041*
*(Dusk) Martin Dee (Exterior & Full
Hall gallery view) Tim Matheson
(Glass lobby & Full Hall ground
view) Don Erhardt*

Fortune Sound Club, *P.088*
(p090 Bottom) Brandon Artis

Guilt & Co., *P.099*
(All) Guilt & Co.

Hastings Racecourse, *P.027*
*(Top) Jockeys and horses racing
by Colin Knowles / CC BY-SA 2.0)
(Bottom) Hastings Racecourse*

Here There, *P.100–101*
*(p102) Josh Nychuk
(p103) Here There*

Lynn Canyon, *P.028–029*
(All) Jaden Nyberg

Museum of Anthropology,
P.046–047
(All) Museum of Anthropology

New Media Gallery, *P.048–049*
(All) New Media Gallery

Osteria Savio Volpe, *P.070–071*
*(All) Knauf and Brown (p073 bot-
tom) IDMG Culinary Marketing,
Mark Kinskofer Photography*

**Presentation House Gallery
(The Polygon Gallery),** *P.039*
*(All) Presentation House Gallery
(The Polygon Gallery)*

Rennie Museum, *P.036–037*
*(P.030, 036 Bottom, 037 middle
left & bottom) Scott Massey (p036
Top) Martin Tessler (P.037 Top &
middle right) Blaine Campbell*

Richmond Night Market, *P.064*
(All) Richmond Night Market

Sea to Sky Gondola, *P.023*
*(P.010, 024–025) Tara Lundrigan
Photography (p023 Top & bottom)*

*Paul Bride (Middle) Tara O'Grady
Photography*

Simon Fraser University,
P.016–017
*(p016 & p017 top left, top right,
bottom) Simon Fraser University
(p017 top left) Damian Moppett,
Large Painting and Caryatid Ma-
quette in Studio at Night (Sculpture Version), 2012. aluminum,
paint, SFU Art Collection. Gift of
the artist. Work commissioned
by the Vancouver Art Gallery
for Offsite (Nov. 8, 2012 – April 1,
2013) with support from the City
of Vancouver and the Michael
O'Brian Family Foundation. (p017
middle right) Guilhem Vellut
(p017 bottom) Bridge Beardslee,
Energy Alignment Sculpture:
Pyramid in the Golden Section,
1976. steel and paint. SFU Art Collection. Gift of Ian Davidson, 1977.*

Sylvia Hotel, *P.014*
(Exterior) Sylvia Hotel

The Acorn, *P.075*
(All) The Acorn

The Aviary, *P.038*
*(Top & bottom) Ema Peter Photog-
raphy (Middle) Bianca Guthrie,
Darian Wong*

The Flats, *P.035*
*(Top left & top right) Courtesy of
Catriona Jeffries*

The Fox Cabaret, *P.098*
(Top & bottom) The Fox Cabaret

Trout Lake Farmers Markets,
P.065
(All) Kaishin Chu

Vancouver Art Gallery, *P.045*
*(Top & middle) Vancouver Art
Gallery*

**Vancouver Convention
Centre West,** *P.018*
*(Top & bottom right) Courtesy of
Vancouver Convention Centre*

Vij's, *P.076*
(Bottom) Vij's

Wildebeest, *P.080–081*
(All) Jonathan Norton
-
*In Accommodation: all courtesy
of respective hotels. The Burred
Hotel, by Martin Tessler*

CITIX60

CITIx60: Vancouver

First published and distributed by
viction workshop ltd

viction:ary™

7C Seabright Plaza, 9-23 Shell Street,
North Point, Hong Kong

Url: www.victionary.com
Email: we@victionary.com
[f] @victionworkshop
[🐦] @victionary_
[◎] @victionworkshop

Edited and produced by viction:ary

Concept & art direction: Victor Cheung
Research & editorial: Queenie Ho, Caroline Kong
Project coordination: Elisabeth Kwan, Katherine Wong
Design & map illustration: MW Wong, Frank Lo

Co-curator & contributing writer: Anna Ling Kaye, Leanne Dunic
Cover map illustration: Janice Wu
Count to 10 illustrations: Guillaume Kashima aka Funny Fun
Photography: Elissa Crowe

Content is compiled based on facts available as of March 2017. Travellers are
advised to check for updates from respective locations before your visit.

First edition
ISBN 978-988-77746-2-4
Printed and bound in China

Acknowledgements

A special thank you to all creatives, photographer(s), editor, producers, companies and organisations for your crucial contributions to our inspiration and
knowledge necessary for the creation of this book. And, to the many whose
names are not credited but have participated in the completion of the book,
we thank you for your input and continuous support all along.